CHOCOLATE CHUNKS

Contents

Tim, the Pest and the Chocolate Robber ..... page 2

Chocolate World ..... page 14

Alison Hawes

Story illustrated by
Ned Woodman

Before Reading

In this story

 Tim

 The Pest

 The chocolate robber

 The shopkeeper

Tricky words

- milk
- basket
- chocolates
- robber
- shopkeeper

Introduce these tricky words and help the reader when they come across them later!

Story starter

Tim lives with his mum and his little sister. His mum is always making him look after his sister. Tim calls her the Pest. One day, Tim's mum asked him to go to the shop.

Tim, the Pest and the Chocolate Robber

Tim had to go to the shop to get some milk.

The Pest wanted to go to the shop, too.

Does Tim want the Pest to go with him?

In the shop, Tim got the milk.

He put the milk in the basket.

The Pest got some chocolates.

She put the chocolates in the basket, too.

"Put the chocolates back!" said Tim.

"No!" said the Pest.

She pulled the chocolates. Tim pulled too.

7

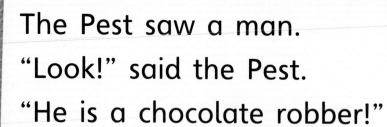

The Pest saw a man.
"Look!" said the Pest.
"He is a chocolate robber!"

She let go of the chocolates.
Tim fell back on to some tins.
"**OW!**" said Tim.

A tin fell on the
chocolate robber.
"**OW!**" said the
chocolate robber.

The shopkeeper got
the chocolate robber.

What will the
shopkeeper say to
Tim and the Pest?

Tim and the Pest got some chocolates!

Quiz

Text Detective

- What did the Pest put in the basket?
- How do you know the shopkeeper was pleased with Tim and the Pest?

Word Detective

- **Phonic Focus:** Final letter sounds
  Page 3: Find a word that ends with 'k'.
- Page 7: Find a word that means 'tugged'.
- Page 9: Find a word with three syllables.

Super Speller

Read these words:

got   put   fell

Now try to spell them!

HA! HA! HA!

Q What's the best thing to put into a chocolate cake?

A Your teeth!

13

Find out about

- Crazy chocolate facts!

Tricky words

- chocolate
- these
- biggest
- world
- chicken
- pizzas
- insects

Introduce these tricky words and help the reader when they come across them later!

Text starter

Do you love chocolate? The world's biggest chocolate bar was as big as a car and some people eat chocolate insects! Do you like chocolate that much?

Chocolate World

Do you love chocolate?
Read these crazy
chocolate facts!

Do you love to eat
big chocolate bars?
These bars are big, but ...

... the biggest chocolate bar
in the world was as big as
a car!

Do you love to eat chocolate eggs?
These eggs are big, but ...

... the biggest chocolate egg in the world was as big as a tree!

People love to eat chocolate. Read *these* crazy chocolate facts!

Some people love to eat chocolate and chicken.

Some people love to eat chocolate pizzas!

Would you eat a chocolate pizza?

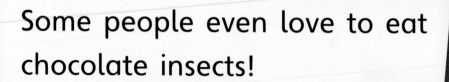

Some people even love to eat chocolate insects!

Do you?

People eat chocolate all over the world. People even eat chocolate in Space!

Quiz

Text Detective

- What is your favourite chocolate?
- Which chocolate recipe would you **not** like to try?

Word Detective

- Phonic Focus: Final letter sounds
  Page 17: Find a word that ends with 'n'.
- Page 16: Find two small words in the word 'these'.
- Page 19: Find a word that ends with 'ee'.

Super Speller

Read these words:

was   in   you

Now try to spell them!

HA! HA! HA!

 Q What did the spaceman say when he stood on the chocolate bar?

A I've just landed on Mars!